LANGUAGE AND WRITING

Miriam Moss

Wayland

Topics

Airports
Ancient Peoples
Archaeology
Bridges
Canals
Castles
Costumes and Clothes
Earthquakes and Volcanoes
Energy
Fairs and Circuses
Farm Animals
Ghosts and the Supernatural
Great Disasters
Helicopters
Houses and Homes
Inventions
Jungles
Language and Writing
Maps and Globes
Money
Musical Instruments
Peoples of the World
Photography
Pollution and Conservation
Prisons and Punishments
Railways
Religions
Robots
Shops
Spacecraft
Stamps
Television
The Age of the Dinosaurs
The Olympics
Trees of the World
Under the Ground
Zoos

All the words that appear in **bold** are explained in the glossary on page 30.

Editor: Elizabeth Clark

Cover: A Japanese child practises calligraphy.

First published in 1987 by
Wayland (Publishers) Ltd
61 Western Road, Hove
East Sussex BN3 1JD, England

British Library Cataloguing in Publication Data

Moss Miriam
Language and writing. – (Topics).
1. Language and languages – Juvenile
I. Title II. Series
400 P124

ISBN 0-85078-830-7

Phototypeset by
Kalligraphics Ltd, Redhill, Surrey
Printed and bound in
Belgium by
Casterman S.A.

Contents

First Languages

Language is a useful way of sending messages. It is a way of telling others about your thoughts and feelings. Animals send messages too. Bees tell each other where they have found nectar. They perform a dance which shows the distance and direction of the nectar from the hive. Geese flying in formation call to each other and whales sing haunting songs as they **migrate** to warm waters.

Wild geese call out to each other as they fly in their striking V-formation.

An aboriginal father gives his child an early lesson in recognizing the names of objects from drawings.

The first people who lived on earth thousands of years ago would have needed to inform each other about what they were doing and feeling. It is thought that at first they would have used grunts, gestures and signs to indicate feelings of anger, surprise or contentment. Later they would have begun to name things – using the same sound to indicate a particular object.

With their system of smoke signals, native North Americans could send messages over long distances.

Linking sound with meaning is the beginning of language. After a time, people began to form rules about how to link up these sounds to express ideas and thoughts, and this was the beginning of **grammar.** Today a young child learns to speak by linking a sound with a particular object and by the age of five will probably be able to use 6,000 words and about 1,000 rules of grammer.

Not all language uses spoken words. Australian aborigines make a clicking sound to talk to each other. They also use message sticks. Notches cut into the sticks act as a kind of code which help the aborigines to remember things. The Incas who lived in Peru long ago used 'quipos'. They knotted wools of different lengths, colours and thicknesses to keep records. Native Americans used smoke signals and African tribes used drum beats to send messages.

It is possible to **communicate** without sounds. Have you seen a clown **miming** in the circus? You can tell a lot about how someone feels by their 'body language' – by the way they stand or sit, or by the expression on their face.

The art of mime uses body language to put its meaning across. What do these clowns think of the skunk in the middle of the picture?

These paintings of hunters were drawn on cave walls by men and women living more than 11,000 years ago.

Another way of communicating is by drawing pictures. Cave paintings and diagrams of animals and huntsmen have been found which were drawn by the people who lived between 15,000 and 11,000 years ago. Later cave paintings show shapes that look like geometric **symbols**. These symbols may have been used to pass on information from one person to another and from one generation to another. This would have been the first form of writing.

How Writing Developed

Writing began when people learned how to pass on information, thoughts and feelings to others by using visible signs. These were understood by the people themselves and others who had been shown what they stood for. Using writing was one of the first signs that a group of people was becoming settled. They used writing to keep records about the land, crops and weather patterns.

These symbols were chipped into the rock in northern Pakistan in the second century AD. They tell stories about the religion in the area.

These pictograms, drawn by Sumerians more than 5,000 years ago, are among the earliest forms of writing.

From about 3,000 BC, people called the Sumerians lived in the valleys of the Tigris and Euphrates rivers. At first they used **pictograms** to give information. These are pictures which communicate a meaning. They were drawn in the soft clay with a sharp stick, or a piece of bone or metal. Gradually, the writing changed into a series of wedge-shaped lines called 'cuneiform writing'.

The ancient Egyptians who lived in the Nile valley between 3,000 and 4,000 BC used a picture language known as **hieroglyphic**. A thousand little symbols of men, birds, plants, feathers and everyday articles were used. Later, the ancient Egyptians combined different signs to form **syllables**. In time, government **scribes** used a quicker, simpler version for ordinary writing, where the pictures were reduced to shapes. This was called **demotic** writing, which looks very like modern Arabic writing. They wrote with reed pens in ink, on paper made from **papyrus.**

Writing was used for important ceremonies. It was sculpted or painted on monuments and tombs. Although we know from these what Egyptian language and writing looked like, we have no idea how it sounded.

When the Greeks invaded Egypt in 322 BC, they brought with them

Ancient Egyptian hieroglyphs. They were known as sacred writings because at first only the priests could write with these symbols.

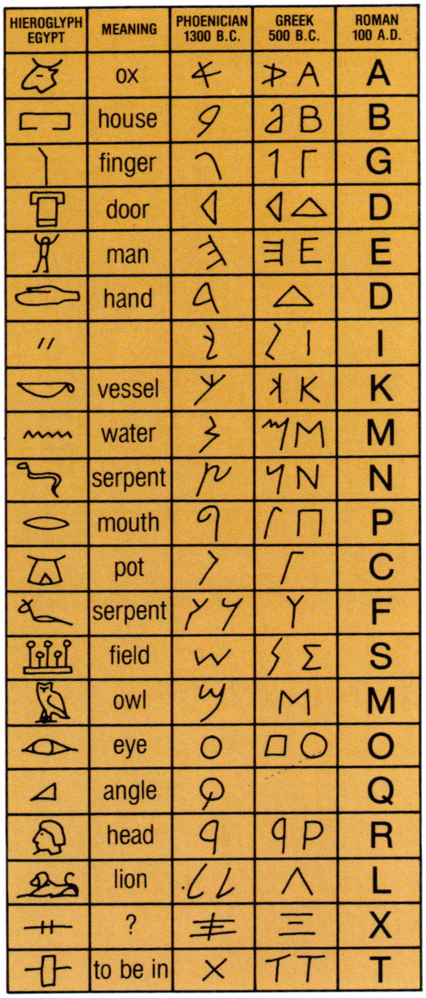

Compare the Egyptian hieroglyph symbols with the Phoenician alphabet and then see how the Roman alphabet developed.

their Greek **alphabet**, which had developed from the **Phoenicians.** The alphabet was a series of symbols which stood for particular sounds. These symbols were combined to make words. There were enough symbols to stand for all the sounds that were needed. A century after the Greeks invaded Egypt, the Egyptian hieroglyphic language had died out. The Greeks were eventually overrun by the Romans, whose empire extended throughout western Europe. The Romans adapted the Greek alphabets. The alphabets of English and many other European languages, are similar to the Roman **script** because of the Roman occupation of Europe, which lasted for 500 years.

The Chinese began writing about 4,000 years ago, during the 'Shang' civilization. At first, animal bones were scratched with pictograms, which were magic symbols.

These were used to foretell the future..By 200 BC the Chinese had combined many of these pictograms, to form new ideas – **ideograms.** Slowly the pictures changed into the very complicated shapes which are used by the Chinese today.

Writing in China has always been considered an art, which is not surprising since modern Chinese has 40,000 **characters** compared to the 26 letters in the English alphabet. Some characters take a long time to write and need as many as 32 strokes of the pen. Chinese poses many problems

日	SUN (jih)	+	一	ONE (j)	=	旦	DAWN (tan)
The sun rising above a flat line representing the horizon means dawn or daybreak.							
門	DOOR (man)	+	口	MOUTH (kloo)	=	問	to ASK (wen)
A mouth in a doorway suggests asking.							
日	SUN (jih)	+	月	MOON (yueh)	=	明	BRIGHT (ming)
The sun combined with the moon means bright.							

Chinese ideograms. You can see how two or more characters standing for simple objects are combined to form new ideas.

This huge, impressive stone calendar was made and used by the Aztec people in Central America.

because it has no alphabet and many people in China today are trying to get their writing made simpler.

Living in Central America between 1325–1500s, the Aztecs used pictograms (known as glyphs) but no alphabet. A written language never developed, which means that the Aztecs relied on memory and speech rather than their writing.

Discoveries

There have been many exciting discoveries about ancient language and writing. Hundreds of clay tablets from what was once the ancient city of Babylon and from Syria have been found in **archaeological** digs. These seem to be the first kind of school books. The neat writing of the teachers is on the left hand side of the tablets and on the right are the children's attempts to copy it.

This is an early scholar's tablet, showing a writing lesson. Do you think the child's writing (on the right) improved with practise?

The discovery of the Rosetta stone was very important because the Greek writing at the bottom was used by scholars to decipher the hieroglyphics at the top.

When students wanted a tablet to write on, they probably took a small handful of clay, flattened it out and wrote on it with a **stylus**. Any mistakes could be smoothed out with the blunt end of the stylus.

The Rosetta stone was discovered in 1799 in Egypt. It shows how the Greek and Egyptian languages were once used at the same time. On the stone is a copy of a law passed by priests in about the year 198 BC. It is inscribed in Egyptian hieroglyphics on the top half. Below this it is written again in demotic characters, and at the bottom it is inscribed in Greek. Experts used the Greek to **decipher** the hieroglyphs at the top. Until then, the meaning of hieroglyphs was unknown to scholars.

In 1947, an Arab boy walking on a hillside above the Dead Sea explored a cave and discovered some old broken jars. In them were ancient manuscripts which proved to be the Bible written in Hebrew in about 100 BC. They became known as the Dead Sea Scrolls.

An archaeologist called Ventris tried to decipher the writing on 600 clay tablets discovered in Greece. There were two sets of tablets of writing arranged in lines (linear) – these were called the Linear A and Linear B tablets. Ventris eventually broke the code of Linear B and found it to be lists and accounts of property in a very old form of Greek writing. The information is in such detail that it could not have been communicated in pictures.

A fragment of the Dead Sea Scrolls showing verses from the Bible written in Ancient Hebrew script.

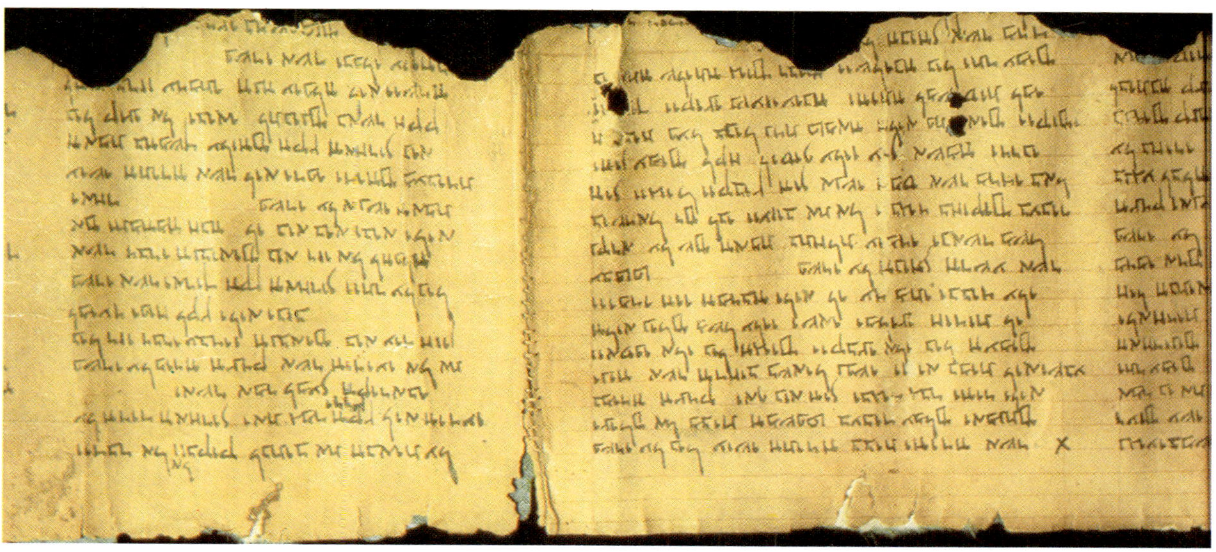

The Phaistos disc from Crete would have been read by turning the disc and following the spiral of symbols.

A clay disc was found at Phaistos in Crete with hieroglyphics impressed upon both sides with a special punch or stamp. This shows that the people who made it must have understood the simplest forms of printing 3,000 years before the invention of printing by moveable type in the fourteenth century.

Paper and Printing

With the invention of the alphabet (see page 12) writing became easier. In most languages the basic characters have not changed much over the last thousand years. Before the invention of printing, in every country there were scribes who were trained to copy rapidly. Many did beautiful work, such as the illuminated **manuscripts** of the Bible done by monks.

Imagine the care that the scribe took when he was decorating this hand-written page with beautiful designs.

An ancient clay statue of an Egyptian scribe showing him in a typical writing pose. You can see the roll of papyrus stretched across his lap.

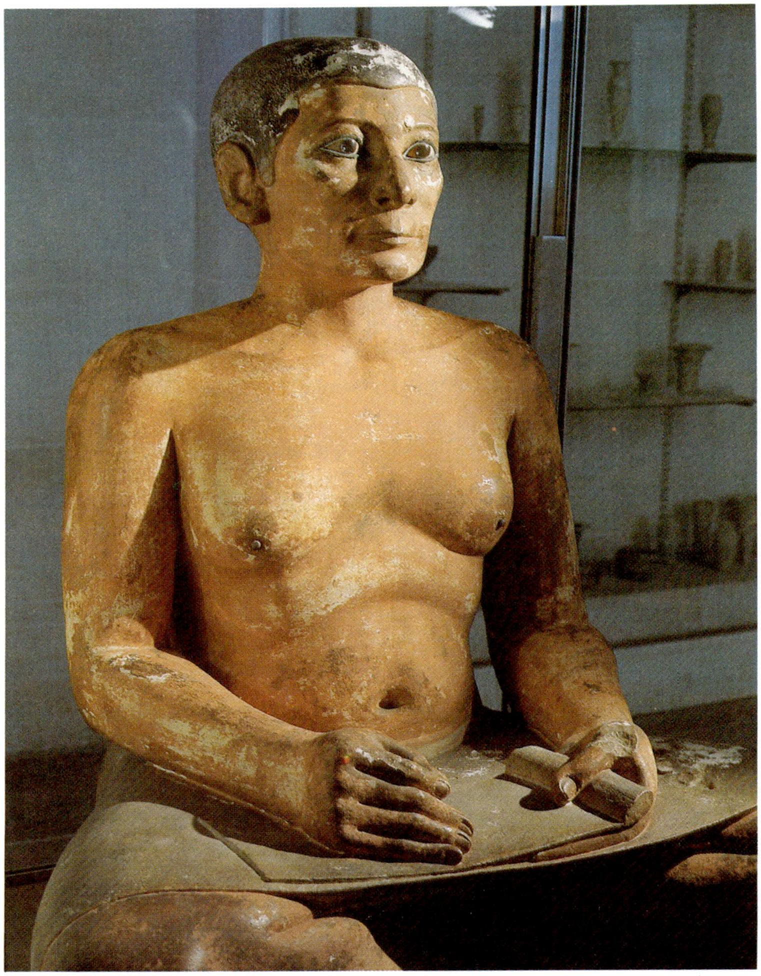

Long rolls of papyrus and **parchment** were written by hand with a brush, reed or **quill**, which was slow, painstaking work. These became the main way of storing information but were expensive. In about AD 300 a sort of book, called a **codex**, began to be used.

Papyrus was still used in parts of the near East until the twelfth century. At the same time paper, up till then used only by the Chinese, came to Europe. The oldest recorded paper **document** in Europe is in Sicily, dated 1102. The use of paper increased and the number of libraries to house the new books grew. One important European library was at a monastery in Monte Cassino, Italy.

The Diamond Sutra, produced in China in AD 868, is the first known printed book.

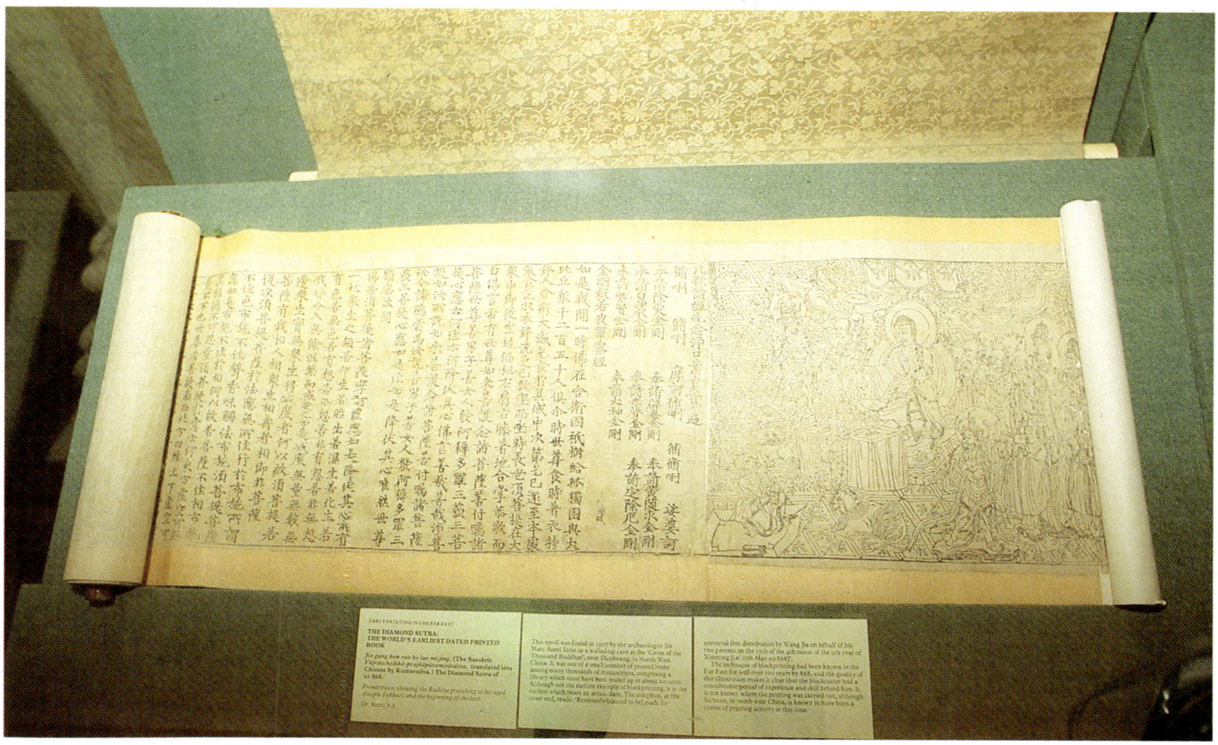

Thomas Caxton, the first printer in Britain, shows his printing press to some royal visitors.

Most libraries in medieval Europe made sure that books were chained to the desks!

The first known printed book was produced in China in AD 868, from wooden blocks coated with ink. By printing on paper, many copies could be produced more cheaply and quickly than ever before.

In 1438, a German called Johannes Gutenberg invented the first mechanical printing press in Europe. The first weekly newspapers, called 'corantos', were published in Europe in 1620.

Different Language Systems

There are now about 5,000 languages in the world. The language spoken by the largest number of people is Mandarin – spoken by 695 million Chinese. English has the most words with 790,000.

Language and writing systems are being invented all the time. Two very important systems are those which enable the deaf and dumb to communicate and the blind to read. Deaf and dumb language systems are based on hand and facial signals. The blind read and write using Braille, a system of raised dots that they understand through touch. Braille is called after its French inventor, Louis Braille.

In the last few hundred years, changes in how we communicate our languages have been rapid.

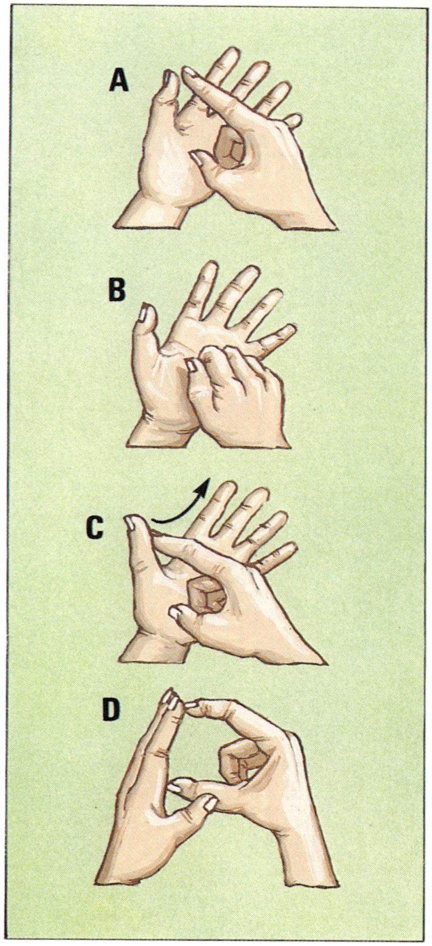

These are the hand-signs used by deaf and dumb people for the first four letters of the alphabet.

This man is sending a message from his computer to a computer in another part of the country.

Now thousands of typewriters, telephones, radios, televisions, **telex** machines and word processors are used in offices, homes and schools all over the world.

In 1962 the first telecommunications satellite sent TV pictures from space. Now hundreds of telecommunications satellites send messages in milliseconds around the globe.

The London Teleport is a satellite earth station in the Docklands.

Do you recognize any of these internationally used pictograms? From top to bottom they are: a sign for the disabled; no smoking; Beware! poison and the Olympic Games symbol.

The results of this are that languages change every day. New words enter languages from other countries as news and the latest ideas in fashion and pop music are transmitted by radio and TV around the earth. Some governments worry about how fast their country's language is changing, and discourage people from using **loan words** from another language. Some countries have government departments to deal with protecting their language. The French are trying to stop too many English words like 'le weekend' from entering their language.

There are many international languages. Pictograms, like those used in road signs, can be read and understood by people of all nationalities. Ships of all nations send messages in the International Code, which is printed in nine main languages. Using this code, messages can be sent quickly by radio, signal-lamp, and by using a siren or flags. Ships also use the international **Morse Code**, in which groups of shorter dots and longer dashes are all signalled to indicate words. There is also a kind of international language used by people who work with computers called 'computerspeak'.

It will be interesting to see how our languages develop in the future, and how many new ones are invented.

A	•▬	S	•••
B	▬•••	T	▬
C	▬•▬•	U	••▬
D	▬••	V	•••▬
E	•	W	•▬▬
F	••▬•	X	▬••▬
G	▬▬•	Y	▬•▬▬
H	••••	Z	▬▬••
I	••	1	•▬▬▬▬
J	•▬▬▬	2	••▬▬▬
K	▬•▬	3	•••▬▬
L	•▬••	4	••••▬
M	▬▬	5	•••••
N	▬•	6	▬••••
O	▬▬▬	7	▬▬•••
P	•▬▬•	8	▬▬▬••
Q	▬▬•▬	9	▬▬▬▬•
R	•▬•	0	▬▬▬▬▬

Above *The Morse alphabet. These signals can be tapped out, or flashed over a distance with light.*

Left *A translator at work behind the scenes at an international conference.*

Perhaps humans will one day learn to communicate with some of the other animals that inhabit the earth. Dolphins have brains as big as ours and their own complicated language of 'clicks' that, as yet, we have failed to understand.

Language may one day be used to communicate with other living creatures that might exist in space. We have already sent messages about ourselves into space.

Perhaps one day we will be able to share the joke with these dolphins in their own language.

With space exploration bringing distant galaxies closer, who knows what forms of life and language we will come across in the future?

In 1972 and 1973 space probes carried picture messages on special metal plates. In 1977 Voyagers 1 and 2 carried earth sounds on phonograph records in the form of a diagram which showed the chemicals of life, a human, our solar system and the radio telescope which sent the message. Will there be a reply, and if so, what kind of language and writing will be used?

Glossary

Alphabet A set of letters or other signs used in writing. The word comes from the names of the first two letters in the Greek alphabet alpha and beta.
Archaeological To do with studying history by looking at ancient ruins.
Characters Symbols used in writing.
Codex A volume of manuscripts of ancient texts.
Communicate To exchange information, ideas or feelings.
Decipher To find out the meaning.
Demotic A simple version of hieroglyphics used by ordinary scribes in ancient Egypt.
Document A paper, booklet, which provides information.
Grammar The rules for how a language is spoken or written.
Hieroglyphic This means 'sacred writings'. Hieroglyphics are symbols used by the ancient Egyptians in their writing.
Ideograms Signs or symbols used in the writing systems of China and Japan to express an idea.
Loan words Words borrowed from other languages.
Manuscripts Books or other documents written by hand.
Migrate To journey between different countries at certain times of the year.
Miming Expressing an idea by using the body and without using words.
Morse Code A telegraph code used internationally for sending messages.
Papyrus A kind of paper made from the stem of a tall water plant found in some hot countries.
Parchment Writing material made from certain animal skins.
Phoenicians An ancient people who lived in what is now north west Syria.
Pictograms Pictures which communicate a meaning.
Quill A feather made into a pen.
Scribes People who made handwritten copies before the invention of printing.
Script Handwriting.
Stylus A pointed tool used for drawing or writing.
Syllables The different sounds that make up a word.

Symbols Something that stands for something else.

Telex An international telegraph service.

Books to Read

For younger readers

Learnabout Codes and Ciphers (Ladybird books Ltd, 1983)

Message Detective by John Satchwell (Walker Books Ltd, 1985)

They lived like this in Ancient Mesopotamia by Maria Neurath and Evelyn Worboys (Max Parrish and Co Ltd, 1964)

They lived like this in the Old Stone Age by Maria Neurath and Muriel Turner (Macdonald and Co, 1970)

The Picture Reference Book of Communications (Brockhampton Press Ltd, 1972)

For older readers

Language and Communication (Cambridge University Press, 1984)

Picture acknowledgements
British Telecom 25; Ed Carr 12; Colorific! 5; Jimmy Holmes 9; Mansell Picture Library 22; Peter Newark's Western Americana 6; Ronald Sheridan 8, 10, 15, 16, 18, 21; Survival Anglia 4; Malcolm Walker 13, 23, 26, 27; Werner Forman 11, 20; ZEFA 7, 14, 17, 24, 27, 28, 29.

Index